Zinnia's Flower Garden

✿ MONICA WELLINGTON ✿

Dutton

Children's Books

New York

To Lucia,
city gardener extraordinaire

ABOUT THE ART
The artwork was made from
color copies of fabrics and photos,
many of which were taken by the author
as she grew the flowers. The color copies
were cut and pasted onto paper painted
with gouache. (The computer was
not used in the preparation
of this artwork.)

Copyright © 2005 by Monica Wellington
All rights reserved.

CIP Data is available.

Published in the United States by Dutton Children's Books,
a division of Penguin Young Readers Group
345 Hudson Street, New York, New York 10014
www.penguin.com/youngreaders

Designed by Gloria Cheng

Manufactured in China · First Edition
ISBN 0-525-47368-8
3 5 7 9 10 8 6 4 2

and to Denis,
with love

Spring has arrived. Zinnia is getting her garden ready for planting. She digs up the soil and turns it over with her shovel. She takes out stones and rakes the dirt smooth. The warm sun feels good as she works.

May 3
Very busy planting my seeds today. Such hard work.

Zinnia carefully plants many kinds of flower seeds in rows. She covers the seeds with dirt and pats it all down very gently. She sprinkles the ground with water.

Cosmos

BLACK-EYED SUSAN

Asters

cosmos seeds

black-eyed Susan seeds

sweet pea seeds

SWEET PEA

aster seeds

May 3
Very busy
planting
my seeds
today. Such
hard work.

Cosmos

BLACK-EYED
SUSAN

Asters

cosmos seeds

black-eyed
Susan seeds

Zinnia carefully plants many kinds of flower seeds in rows. She covers the seeds with dirt and pats it all down very gently. She sprinkles the ground with water.

sweet pea seeds

SWEET PEA

aster seeds

cumulus cloud

cirrus cloud

nimbus cloud

stratus cloud

Zinnia waits for the seeds to sprout.
The seeds need the sun to shine,
the rain to fall, and many days to
pass. It is hard to wait so long for
her seeds to grow.

°C
40
30
20
10
0

°F
100
90
80
70
60
50
40
30
20

May 12
Rain all day—
Ugh! But it
is good for
my garden.

Every day Zinnia checks her garden to see if anything has happened. Look! The first seedling is poking its way up through the dirt.

stages of germination

May 20
My first sprout today. WOW!

May 29
Lots of sprouts now.
I can't even count them all.

Now Zinnia's garden is full of green sprouts growing toward the sun. Little stems grow taller. Little leaves get bigger. Little roots burrow deeper into the earth.

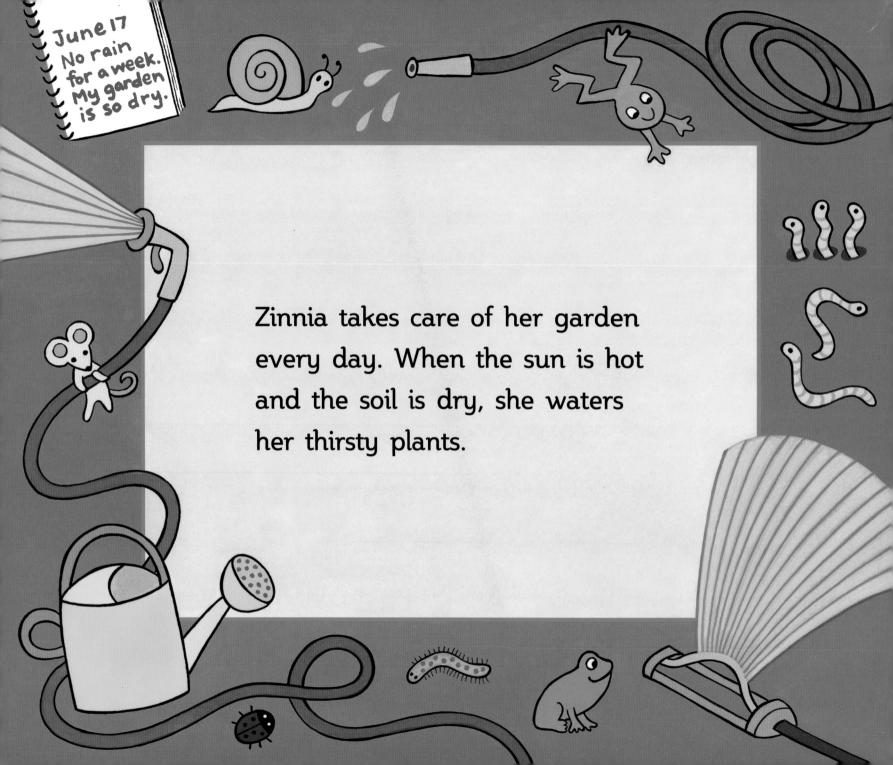

June 17
No rain
for a week.
My garden
is so dry.

Zinnia takes care of her garden
every day. When the sun is hot
and the soil is dry, she waters
her thirsty plants.

July 7
My sun-
flower
plants are
so tall.

I HATE
weeds!

She pulls up pesky weeds that try to crowd out her plants. She inspects them for greedy bugs. She measures how tall her strong and healthy plants are growing. Every day they get bigger and bigger.

First thing in the morning, Zinnia runs out to check her garden. She is excited to see little buds growing on many of her plants.

July 18
My zinnias have buds. I wonder what color they are going to be?

Life Cycle of the Butterfly

eggs

caterpillar

chrysalis

adult

ready to fly

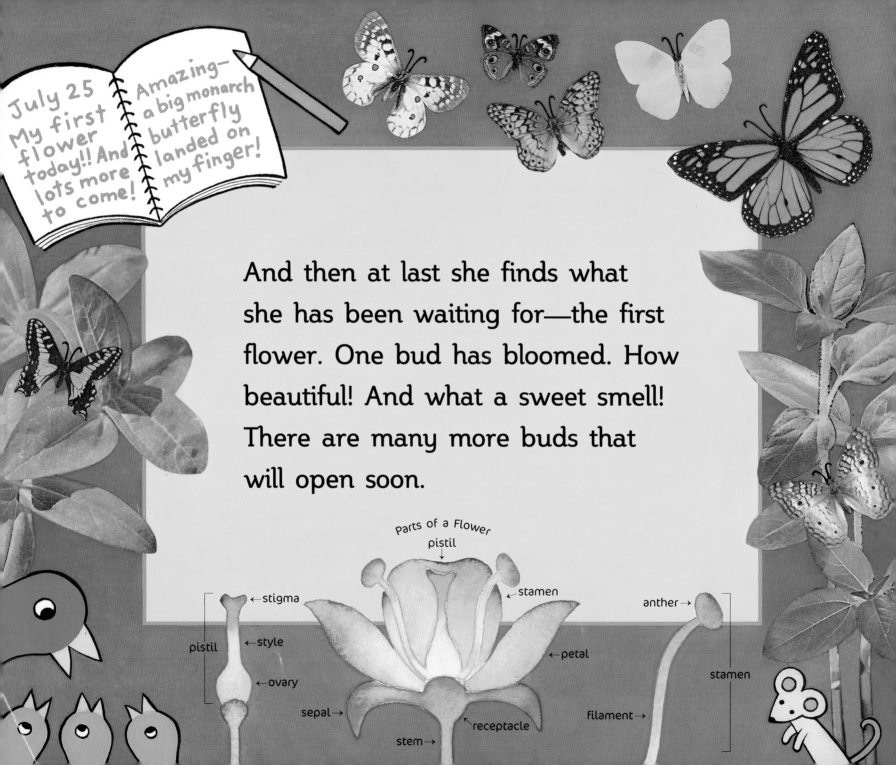

July 25
My first
flower
today!! And
lots more
to come!

Amazing—
a big monarch
butterfly
landed on
my finger!

And then at last she finds what she has been waiting for—the first flower. One bud has bloomed. How beautiful! And what a sweet smell! There are many more buds that will open soon.

Parts of a Flower

pistil

←stigma

pistil

←style

←ovary

sepal→

stem→

←receptacle

stamen

←petal

anther→

filament→

stamen

The garden grows and grows with blossoming flowers. Zinnia paints, reads, and picnics among them. Butterflies flutter. Bees buzz. Zinnia's garden is her favorite place to be on these warm summer days.

August 11
I LOVE MY GARDEN!

sunflower

snapdragon

zinnia

black-eyed Susan

sweet pea

marigold

cosmos

sweet William

aster

Her flowers are abundant, and Zinnia cuts some to arrange into bouquets. The fragrant scents of the flowers swirl around her in the warm breeze.

August 21
My sunflowers
are taller
than I am!

25 + 25 + 25 + 25 = $1

5 5 5 5 + 5 5 5 5 + 5 5 5 5 + 5 5 5 5 + 5 5 5 5 = $1

10 10 10 10 10 10 10 10 10 10 = $1

One hot summer day, Zinnia has a lemonade stand and puts up a sign: Pick your own FLOWERS. Customers come and gather bunches of flowers and drop money in her jar.

August 28
Busy today
at my stand.
Everyone
loves my
flowers!

Don't forget to smell the FLOWERS!

stigma→

maturing ovary

growing seed

←stamen

sepal→

petal

↑
stem

In the autumn, as it gets colder, Zinnia picks the last flowers from her garden. She finds ripe seeds that have formed. They are ready to be collected. She will save them to plant next year.

October 13
Lots of seeds!
(I'll leave some for the birds.)

From Flower to Seed

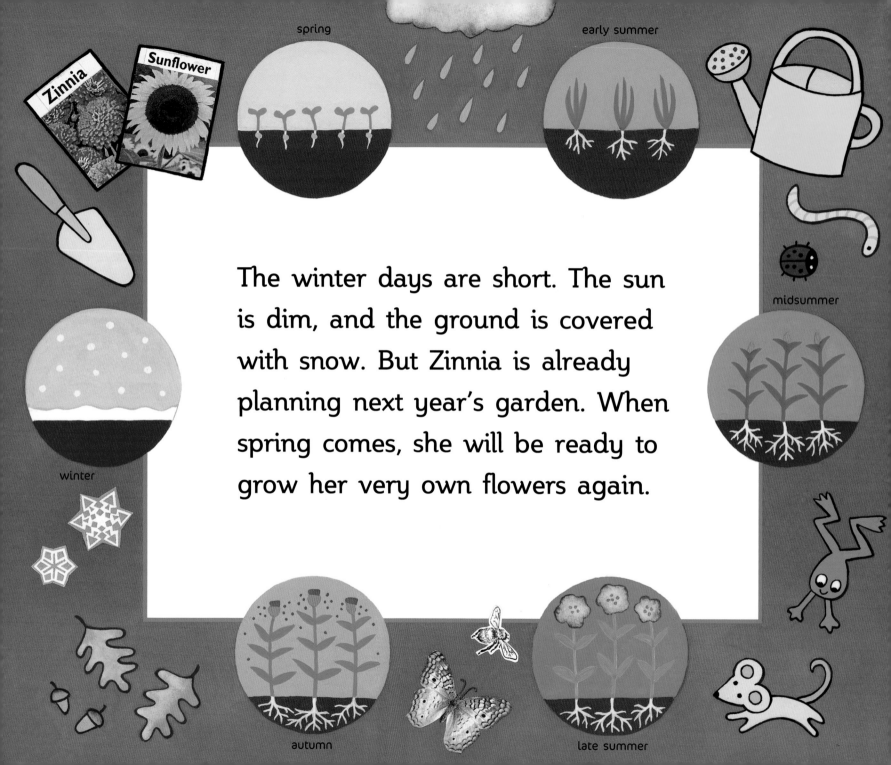

spring

early summer

midsummer

winter

autumn

late summer

The winter days are short. The sun is dim, and the ground is covered with snow. But Zinnia is already planning next year's garden. When spring comes, she will be ready to grow her very own flowers again.

Zinnia

Sunflower

GROWING YOUR OWN FLOWERS

It is easy to turn tiny seeds into big beautiful flowers. Just follow these steps:

✿ You can start your seeds outside in the ground, like Zinnia did, or indoors in containers. Use a cup, milk carton, or clay pot. Be sure you cut holes in the bottom of the container so that water can drain out.

✿ Soak the seeds overnight, just before planting, so they will sprout more quickly.

✿ Fill your containers with prepared dirt.

✿ Plant a few seeds in each container, leaving space between each seed. Cover with a little bit of soil, following the directions on the seed packets.

✿ Label each container with the name of the flower you planted.

✿ Water the seeds and place the containers in a sunny spot.

✿ Check the soil every day. Keep it moist.

✿ Indoors, the seeds will probably sprout in two to ten days.

✿ When the seedlings are a bit bigger, you can transplant them outdoors into your garden. Or if you are going to keep them indoors, make sure your containers are big enough for the plants as they grow bigger.

✿ If you take good care of your plants, they will bloom in two to three months. Then you will have beautiful flowers—just like Zinnia!